CARING AND COPING
WHEN YOUR LOVED ONE
IS SERIOUSLY ILL

 BC Cancer Agency
CARE & RESEARCH

While the BC Cancer Agency considers this information to be useful, it may vary from our standard practice and protocol.

It is intended for educational purposes only and should not be substituted for the advice of a healthcare professional.

CARING AND COPING WHEN YOUR LOVED ONE IS SERIOUSLY ILL

Earl A. Grollman

BEACON PRESS   *BOSTON*

Beacon Press
25 Beacon Street
Boston, Massachusetts 02108-2892

Beacon Press books are published under the auspices
of the Unitarian Universalist Association
of Congregations.

05 04 03 02   7 6 5 4 3

Library of Congress Cataloging-in-Publication Data

Grollman, Earl A.
    Caring and coping when your loved one is seriously ill /
Earl A. Grollman.
        p. cm.
    Rev. ed. of In sickness and in health.
    ISBN 0-8070-2713-8
    1. Critically ill—Family relationships. 2. Terminally ill—
Family relationships. 3. Consolation. I. Grollman, Earl A.
In sickness and in health. II. Title.
R726.8.G76   1995
155.9′37—dc20   94-38771

*This book is lovingly dedicated to
Anne and Ray Loewen and
The Loewen Foundation for Children
whose support for terminally ill children
is an inspiration to us all.*

Contents

What this book is about . . .

Someone in your family or a close friend is suffering from serious illness. This has an upsetting and disruptive effect not only on the sick person, but on the family and friends as well.

You may say: "I never imagined it could be like this."

The purpose of this book is to assist you in moving from helplessness to helpfulness; to help you cope with your own emotional upheaval; and better understand the needs of your loved one.

CARING AND COPING
WHEN YOUR LOVED ONE
IS SERIOUSLY ILL

1

IMPACT AND GRIEF

*Your Needs When
Your Loved One
Is Seriously Ill*

*If you want life,
expect pain.*

—MARTIN BUBER

Your loved one is very sick.

You feel as though you have fallen
into a dark pit,
separated from everyone and everything.

My God, my God,
Why hast Thou forsaken me?
I cry by day,
but Thou dost not answer,
and by night,
but find no rest.
                        —Psalm 22

Time stands still.
The real seems so unreal.

You want to cry out
But your throat is tight.

Your lips move.
But no sound comes forth.

Your body is frozen.

A huge stone has settled in
your stomach.

Gradually,
emotions rush over you,
invading and holding you
in the grip of
anger and anguish,
fear and frustration,
dread and despair.

You are afraid
you will lose control,
be swept away by
overpowering emotions.

You keep repeating:

"My loved one is sick.
My loved one is sick.
My loved one is sick,"

as if the sounds
of these frightening words
will enable you to
understand and accept
the terrifying truth.

But speech brings
little comfort or consolation.

You are in
excruciating pain.

The sting of serious illness
is real.

You fear
that your loved one
may never recover.

Loss of health
squeezes the life out of you.

The more your life is bound up
with your beloved
the more vulnerable you are
to grief.

You can't imagine the fact that your beloved
will not be able to share
your life together
in the way you once knew.

You want your lives
to be as before

dreams came crashing down.

"I wish I were sick instead."

Why pretend that you are not experiencing
difficult feelings
during painful moments?

Is it because you feel
so vulnerable?

Is it because
you are afraid of the reactions of others?

Have you been taught
that being strong
means *not* to show feeling?

It is *normal* to grieve.

When a loved one is in poor health,
it's like losing a part of your self.

You have
a deep personal investment in your relationship.

You don't want to lose it.

Grief is an adaptive
response to loss.

Social scientists call it
"anticipatory" or "preparatory grief"—
the working through of your sorrow
as a rehearsal for a doubtful future.

Your anticipation and preparation
help you to
understand and cope
with the impact of your possible loss.

You have every right
to feel the weight of depression.

You grieve
because
you love.

You feel like a victim
of a sudden windstorm—
swept away by forces
you didn't expect and
can't control.

Not everyone will understand
your needs.

Some people may say to you,
"Don't be depressed,"
 or
"Don't act so angry."

Some people will
feel uncomfortable
with your frustration and unhappiness.

But rest assured:
your grief is a normal process
of waves and sensations
that spin you around
in an emotional whirlpool.

How you confront your feelings
depends upon so many factors:

the way you normally handle stress,
the severity of your loved one's illness, and
the support of your friends, medical staff,
and family.

Even though grief is
a common human experience,
it is as individual
as fingerprints—
appearing in
widely varying combinations.

As you experience
some of the emotions associated
with grief,
you may feel like a cork bobbing erratically
on a sea of conflicting emotions.

Unreality

You hear the diagnosis of the illness
but don't feel it.

You cry in a detached way
devoid of any sense
of what is happening
to your loved one
and to you.

You feel numb.

An initial phase of grief
is a sense of unreality,
serving as a built-in buffer
to help you weather the storm.

Numbness affords a respite—
an emotional suspension—
before you go forward
to accept the crushing news
of your loved one's sickness.

Disbelief

If you accept reality,
you might have to exchange
your numbness for pain.

It's hard to accept things
you don't want to be true.

"I *can't* believe it."
"I *won't* believe it."
"I *don't* believe it."

"There might be some mistake.
The medical reports are mixed up
with someone else's.

We'll get a second opinion
—or a third—

There *must* be something
they can do."

You dream at night,
that your loved one is healthy,
just fine.

You take every small improvement
as a sign that your loved one
is now better.
"God wouldn't let this
happen to me *now!*"

Just as you may close your eyes
when something offends your sight,
so are you now refusing to accept

what your mind knows to be true.

Denial isn't
an all-or-nothing affair.

You may have moments of acceptance
when you think about the severity of the illness.

Alternately,
there could be disbelief
as you plan for
the far-off future—*together*,
just as before.

"This is a nightmare.
Please let me wake up
and find things just as they were before."

Fantasies make acceptance
a slow process.

But eventually you will be able to say,
"My loved one is very sick."

This admission is a
landmark
in your journey.

Panic

Acceptance, though, doesn't always
bring peace.
"Why can't I get hold of myself?"

Your physical and emotional
resources are stretched to the limit.

You feel like
you are losing control.

You feel helpless and disorganized.

"If only I could run away,
anywhere."

You need time to
collect yourself.

Hostility

When
    a mother's beauty fades,
    a strong father becomes frail,
    a child's hair falls out,

your sense of helplessness may turn to rage.

"Why me?
Why my beloved?
What did *we* do to deserve this?"

You may be infuriated with
the doctors and nurses,
    for not doing more,
the clergy,
    whose intervention has failed,
God,
    for being unjust,
friends and neighbors,
    who seem healthy and happy.

You may even be angry with your loved one,
for becoming gravely ill
and spoiling future plans.

And you are furious with yourself
for feeling furious.

Your nerves are constantly on edge.
Little things disturb you.

Anger comes unexpectedly and
is hard to contain.
You feel a lingering bitterness.

"I don't deserve this."

Rage
helps you to release
your anguish and frustration
at your inability
to *do* something about it.

Holding back your anger too much
can lead to a deep depression.

Depression

Your emotions are beaten down.
You have the sickening feeling
of going down, down, down.

Silence in solitude
is preferable to the burden of
socializing with friends.

You feel overwhelmed—drained.

Nothing matters anymore.
Nothing.

"Life will *never* be worth living."

Depression colors
everything you do and think.

Hopelessness
hangs around your neck
like an albatross.

Every cloud does *not* have a silver lining.
When there is inner and outer turmoil,
no cloud has a silver lining.

Depression is anger turned inward,
a kind of frozen rage.

It is not only a normal response to anticipated
loss,
but a psychological necessity
for working through your pain.

Now you are facing reality.
You are suffering.
The truth *has* registered.
The signs are impossible to ignore.
Your loved one is in poor health.

And you have started to despair.

Bargaining

You no longer deny your loved one is ill.
But *maybe* you can stave it off,
if you make a deal.

"I'll be more charitable.
Read the Bible.
Give up smoking.

Just let my beloved be as before
until
our anniversary . . . our daughter's graduation
. . . our son's wedding.

I'll never ask for another favor again."

These bargains, usually kept secret,
are your attempts to
improve the terms
of a contract with destiny, fate, or God.

As a reward for your good behavior,
the sickness will be reversed.

You hope.

Magical agreements have nothing
to do with the sickness
or health
of another person.

Even if you keep your
promises (and most people don't),
you can't change the
course of the illness.

Guilt

You may be searching in your heart
for ways you have failed your loved one,
accusing yourself of negligence.

You may even lay the blame
for the illness
on an indiscretion or act
that occurred *before* the illness.

One man confided his
terrible feelings of recrimination—
attributing his wife's cancer
to his infidelity.

You may unrealistically
assume a power and
control
you simply do not possess.

You are suffering a guilt
that denies what you are—

a fallible, normal human being.

You can't learn to love
unless you are willing to run the risk
of offending and failing.

You cannot love deeply
without occasionally hurting
the person you love.

All of us say and do things
we later regret.

There is always something more
we could have done.

Sometimes we *may* feel responsible
for causing the illness—
through poor diet or because
we pushed too hard—

but in most cases
nothing that you did
could have caused
illness in another.

Plaguing yourself with guilt
will not
make you or
your loved one better.

The fact that you may
blame yourself
demonstrates a concern
and a capacity
to feel for another.

Physical Distress

Anxiety and fear create physical pain.

Your mind can cause
changes in the way
your body works.

Your feelings churn,
your stomach aches.

Food may have little taste
for you.

You eat only
because you think you should—
or you are pushed
to do it.

Or else
you can't stop eating.

You constantly crave
a sugar or carbohydrate "fix"
to ease
an insatiable emotional hunger,
to make your grief
more manageable.

You might also experience
long and torturous nights,
   an inability to sleep,
respiratory upsets,
   constant colds and sore throats.

Perhaps you have some of the symptoms
of your loved one's illness.

You feel worn out and bedraggled.

Your body *is* feeling
the emotional loss.

The pain is not imagined.
It is *real*.

Strain adds to *your* risk
of ill health.

Check with your physician.
Have a physical examination.

If you can share with your doctor
not only your medical problems but
your emotional feelings and fears—
your bodily distress
may begin to diminish.

Tears

"I can't stop crying.
Am I losing control of myself?"

No.
You have every reason to weep.

Tears help to release emotions,
unlocking the tensions inside you.

Each person grieves in
his or her own way.

If you don't cry,
it should not be labeled
as "strength" or "bravery."

If you do cry,
it should not be described
as "weakness" or "cowardice."

Tears are a healthy, normal way
of coping.

They affirm your grief.

Intellectualization

Instead of emotional release,
often there are
words,
theories,
philosophical speculations.

Clinical and technical expressions
can cover up
your own real, intimate responses.

Certainly use information
for self-analysis.

But do not suffer paralysis
through analysis.

Reprieve

After you have begun to realize
the gravity of the illness,
your beloved takes a turn for the better.
You are unprepared.

You may have *already* withdrawn
a part of yourself and
accepted the reality of the sickness.

There are mixed feelings.

Unsettled as you are by confused emotions,
you are coming to terms with the loss of health,
understanding
that there is

no day without night, and

no hope without despair.

As you better *understand* yourself,
your anxiety and anguish,
as you begin to *accept* yourself,
even in your own insecurity,

you are better able to
understand and *accept*
your loved one's illness
and respond to his or her needs.

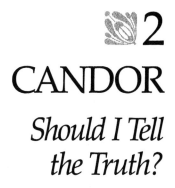

2

CANDOR

Should I Tell the Truth?

<blockquote>
*"I never thought
she could handle it.
But now she knows
the prognosis, she is
so much more at peace . . .
and we can really talk."*

—A HUSBAND
</blockquote>

"I can't possibly tell my loved one
how sick he is.
It would destroy him.
He can't possibly handle
this terrible prognosis."

Maybe it is
you,

not your beloved,
who can't handle
and share the truth.

The question is not
whether or not
to tell of the
seriousness of the illness,

but

who shall tell,
how to tell,
what to tell,
and *when.*

There are so many
games people play:
"You're doing so well."
"Let's not talk about it."
"You'll live to be a hundred."

Avoidance, fatalism, changing the subject,
denial, reassurance—
all erect barriers to communication.

Games are usually played
for the healthy people's sake,
not for the benefit of the person who is ill.

Your loved one probably knows
more than you think.

You communicate
so much nonverbally.

You disclose information
by facial expressions,
your mood,
defensiveness, and
avoidance.

Patients may learn of their conditions
from cues by the hospital staff,
ranging in subtlety from
nurses' anxious glances and avoidance to
overhearing a discussion of the case
by doctors outside the doorway.

Patients often sneak a glance
at their progress reports.

Nor are they fooled about
drastic changes in their bodies.

They know that
radical surgery
is not performed for trivial reasons, and
radiation therapy
is not administered for benign diseases.

Their bodies may be impaired
but
their minds are not.

Even children sense fairly accurately
the trend of their illness.

They know they are unwell
when they have less
energy, appetite,
enthusiasm.

Through their drawings and behavior
they let *us* know
that something traumatic
is happening to *them*.

Children who are very sick use symbolic
language
to reveal their inner concerns.

A little girl expressed her anxiety
by drawing a picture of a child
locked in a room.

One boy with cystic fibrosis
painted a small child in a boat
crashing into the rocks,
sinking.

Another youngster drew a picture
of a crib
that looked like a prison.

When people of all ages
do not share their feelings and fears vocally,
their silence may not be denial,
or lack of understanding of their situation,

but the attempt to conceal their awareness
from friends and family who,
they believe, *can't* handle
an emotional confrontation,

and even from doctors and nurses
who might become annoyed and irritable.

The sick person becomes the
protector and caretaker
of the healthy.

What a burden that must be!

Your loved one
probably wants to know the truth.

Most patients wish to know their diagnosis,
whatever it is
so they can actually participate in their treatment,
read about the latest medical advances,
question the doctors
about their treatment and prognosis.

Many physicians prefer
to withhold this information.
And yet most of them reveal that
they would want to be told.

When ailing people
are informed of their condition
they generally suffer
no negative consequences.

When they are *not* told the truth,

they are deprived
of free expression and
shared understanding.

Because of the conspiracy of silence,
they cannot express their fears and anxieties
and be comforted.

They are "managed" like children,
stripped of self-determination and control.

Awareness opens communication
and allows choice;

choice encourages rational thinking;
rational thinking reduces
the fear of the unknown.

The American Hospital Association
Patients' Bill of Rights
includes this:

The patient has the right to obtain
from his physician complete current
information concerning his diagnosis,
treatment, and prognosis in terms the
patient can be reasonably expected to understand
. . . to give informed consent
prior to the start of any procedure
. . . and to refuse treatment
to the extent permitted by law.

Who Should Tell?

Usually the family physician,
but *never* on the telephone
(which occurs all too frequently).

Choose a time
when you can sit down
to talk together
without outside distraction.

After you hear the diagnosis,
share your understanding of the illness,
your reactions, fears, and feelings
about the condition, and
discuss the nature of the treatment.

There are no silly questions
when a loved one is seriously ill.

How to Tell

You hope your doctor will speak
simply,
gently,
balancing candor with kindness.

You or your loved one may hear the words
"stroke" or "heart disease"
and hear nothing else.

Later, when you are alone together,
try to recall and
clarify what you heard.

Be careful not to shut out your loved one
because you are so pained.

Another doctor's appointment may be scheduled
after you both have a chance
to absorb the bitter news.

Especially during difficult moments,
repetition
brings clarification and reinforcement.

What to Tell

The truth.
But truth is relative.

Some people can absorb it
only in small amounts.

Be sensitive to what your loved one
is or is not
asking.

People ordinarily do not face their serious illness
with any more objectivity or serenity
than they have shown
during other life crises.

Nor should they be told in a way
that completely extinguishes hope.

But the hope must
be anchored in
realistic possibilities.

To speak of a cure
when there is no cure
encourages false hope.

But their
pain *may* be reduced.
The life span *may* be extended
even beyond the doctor's expectations.

Frankness does not mean hopelessness.

Hope means different things
for different people
at different times.

Cancer patients hope before
the diagnosis
it won't be true.

But when it is,
they hope
they won't have too much pain.

And finally they may hope only
they'll live to see
a grandchild born.

Each hope is realistic—for the time.
Each hope is tailored
to the new reality.

The greatest hope
is for your loved one to live
as comfortably—as usefully—
as normally—as possible:
to be valued, and
to be loved,
in the setting of
his or her choice.

3

YOUR LOVED ONE'S NEEDS

*"No, my legs don't work
so well anymore, but
I can still think.
Everyone acts as though my
mind is crippled."*

—A PERSON WITH
MULTIPLE SCLEROSIS

Your loved one is *also*
in the throes
of anguish and agony.

It is a very understandable sorrow.

He or she is in poor health.

Your Loved One's Emotional Needs

The emotional requirements
of your loved one
may be harder
to understand and
tend to
than physical needs.

After all,
there are emotional consequences:
of treatments like chemotherapy and
radiation;
of the financial drain of continual care;
and maybe of thinking
"Death is better than this kind of life."

The possibility of losing social acceptance,
a sense of identity, and
a sense of dignity
is a real fear.

What torment it can be.

When an Illness Is Incurable: A Breach of Etiquette

A person with a malady that is inoperable
may be ignored
by hospital personnel.

Priority is often given
to those whom they
might cure.

When doctors and nurses—
even family and friends—
see little hope for the patient's improvement,
they may withdraw from the patient,
treating the diseased organs
but not the person.

The seriously ill can be placed in
a state of isolation,
treated as lepers.

The people who are this sick
are often cast into limbo,
depersonalized and dehumanized.

This only confirms their
deep-seated fears of
helplessness, hopelessness, and
abandonment.

Friends and family may say:
"I won't visit today.
It might be too tiring for my loved one.
Rest is so important."

It's one thing for a person
to *choose* to be alone.

It's quite another
to be *left* alone.

Ailing people, too, crave
companionship,
social acceptance, and
especially
emotional *warmth*.

They may see themselves
as rejected and discarded.

Often they *are!*

But they are afraid to share
their depression.

Family and friends may say
how well they're doing.
If patients respond with
the truth—
"I'm not doing well at all"—

will their loved ones come back?

Loneliness may be more
fearsome
than even pain.

A Sense of Identity

When family and friends retreat,
your loved one may have doubts
about his or her significance
and self-worth.

"I used to be a healthy
parent,
  brother,
    sister,
      spouse,
        child,
          friend,
            person."

Relationships affirm identity.

"What am I now?
Do my family, friends, the hospital staff
see me only as
a sick patient who may never again be as well?"

"Yes, I'm ill
But I'm not dead yet.
I'm still a living, breathing person
with integrity and self-esteem.
I need to be liked for myself.
I need to live while I'm still alive."

A Sense of Dignity

"That means recognizing my needs
for self-worth,
to live my life the way *I* want,
as usefully and
as normally
as possible."

When there is a serious illness,
family members may mistakenly believe
that their loved one
is no longer lucid and
is unable to discuss family matters,

or
even to make decisions
about his or her own health care.

In your zeal to protect your loved one
from "unnecessary stress"
you may say:
"Don't worry.
Everything is being taken care of."

Your beloved is experiencing
a "premortem" death.

There is no dignity
when a *living* person
is left
for *dead*.

Allow your loved one to do the things
he or she *can* do,
and give encouragement
to do things
he or she *doesn't think* are possible.

Let your actions be based
on your beloved's needs,
not only on your own.

One person
wore a jersey in the hospital that read,

"Be patient,
God isn't finished with me yet."

As people
are able to recognize and resolve
many of their inner conflicts,
they become more at ease
with the idea of the seriousness of the illness.

They are more able
to face the prospect of their sickness
with a sense of
acceptance and peace,

as long as
their physical needs
are also met.

Your Loved One's Physical Needs

Life encompasses mind, spirit, and *body*.

Total care
means not only emotional comfort,
but control and relief of physical distress.

Good medical help is essential.

A Proper Diagnosis

The eminent psychiatrist Dr. Karl Menninger
asked his medical students for the most
significant part of the treatment process.

Some pupils referred to the skills
of the surgeon,
a few to bedside manner,
others to the revolution in drug therapy.

Dr. Menninger rejected all their answers.

His response was "a proper diagnosis."

If a patient is not correctly diagnosed,
he or she cannot be helped.

Many doctors have amazing skills and
knowledge in some areas.
But their wisdom may not extend to
all aspects of medical care.

The physician is an M.D.,
not an M-Deity.

Very often the least-used words
in medicine are:
    "I don't know."
    "Let's find out."
    "I know where we might go to
      get some answers."

Don't be embarrassed
to ask for a consultation
with another doctor.

But *beware* of changing physicians regularly, or
flying around the country to assorted clinics.
This may demonstrate your *own* denial of the
illness,
and could prevent your loved one
from participating in a consistent course of
treatment.

A Caring Physician

The word *diagnosis* derives from the Greek
gignōskein—to know, and *dia*—through and
through.

Choose a physician who will *know*
your loved one
as *through* and *through* as possible.

A health professional who will
STOP,
   LOOK, and
      LISTEN.

A doctor who will

stop
to talk to you and your loved one,
not just walk into the room,
stand over your beloved for a brief moment,
mumble some technical phrases, and then
abruptly retreat;

look
at himself or herself with honesty as a physician,
not hiding behind the mask of professionalism,
admitting feelings of uncertainty, and
not threatened by the limitations
of medicine to cure,

and *listen*
to what you and your loved one
have to say, and
not treat you as irresponsible children.

A secure, caring physician allows
and encourages
participation in meaningful decisions.

Obviously, just as there are
no all-perfect people,
so there can be
no all-perfect physician.

A doctor who meets
the need of one person splendidly
can be ineffectual
with another.

Determine with your family physician
which specialist
would give your loved one
the medical care that is needed
and would understand as well
your beloved's
likes and dislikes,
concerns and fears,
hopes and desires—

who would know the patient as a person.

Control of Pain and Suffering

Pain is not only physical,
it is psychological as well.

Whether pain is bearable
may depend upon the meaning
a person gives to it.

Everyone has a
different
tolerance for pain.

Drug therapy is often administered
to relieve suffering.

New discoveries in pharmacology
help many patients
live with their illness
without torment,
and sometimes even without discomfort.

The patients often know
their *own* need for drugs.

Too often medicines are given
before they are requested,
before they are needed.

Drugs should not be administered
so as to distort reality or
alter the state of consciousness.

Using drugs for the convenience
of the staff
is *drug abuse.*

Speak to your doctor.

Share your observations
of your loved one's response to the medication
and inquire
whether the dosage is appropriate
for your loved one's *present* condition and
whether other drugs
or none at all
may *now* be indicated.

The purpose of the medication
is to make patients' lives
as bearable as possible,
and help them to go on living
as themselves.

Treatment can become overtreatment.

To artificially prolong life
with heroic measures, when
the pain is great, and
death is imminent,

may not be in the best interest
of your loved one.

Sick people, too, demand dignity.

4

YOUR
CHILDREN'S
NEEDS

*"Why won't they
let me see my
grandpa?"*

—A SEVEN-YEAR-OLD

83•

You are not the only one affected
by sickness in the family.

Children are often forgotten by grieving adults.

Having a loved one who is seriously ill
is potentially destructive to their health.

Sickness leaves an imprint on
the healthiest of personalities.

Be truthful.

Explain to your youngsters,
in words they can understand,
what the problem is,
why you are not as available to them as before,
and why your moods are so changeable.

Silence and secrecy
heighten their sense of being shut out
and isolated
from reality.

If possible,
encourage them to visit, too.
They are part of the family.

You will be surprised at the
cheering effect they will
have on your loved one.

The role of children
can be pivotal
in a sick person's ability
to feel vital and alive.

Prepare them in advance
for what the person will look like—
with bandages or sores or hair and weight loss,
with tubes, a respirator, or
other medical equipment.

Children need not be harmed emotionally
by visiting the seriously ill.

What they see is rarely so bad
as what they fear might be.

They may learn that mental health
is not the denial of tragedy,
but the frank acknowledgment of it.

A visit can prepare them for the future.

5
SETTINGS

*"I have lived almost all my life
in this house
and this is where
I want to be."*

—A TERMINALLY ILL PATIENT

Years ago, most people were nursed at home,
and died there.

Periods of illness
took place in the midst of kin,
with the comfort of familiar surroundings.

Today most people are placed
in institutions.

The French social historian Philippe Ariès
describes the trend as
"a brutal revolution in traditional ideas
and feelings."

Most people
would choose to be at home,
in an environment of continuity and security,
having the greatest possible control
over their lives,

not treated just as ailing patients,
but as human beings.

Many ill people and their families
are unaware
that being at home
can be a real option.

There are resources.
Hospital outpatient departments,
medical and nursing services
can provide help for
your beloved at home.

Relatives and friends can be taught
how to care effectively for the loved one and
how to administer drugs at home.

Homemaker and sitter services
will allow you some respite
from constant care.

You may benefit, too,
if you care for your
loved one.

You are giving a gift of
your time,
your self,
your familiar touch.

Sharing your
burdens, joys, and hours together
may draw you closer
and ease your sense
of helplessness and guilt.

Institutions can distance sick people
when
they may spend their days
in sterile settings,
sharing accommodations with strangers,
managed by institutional personnel
rather than family.

Often they live lonely existences,
neither dignified nor tranquil.

The bureaucratization of serious illness
can have a high psychological cost.

But home care is
not always possible or desirable.

Don't feel guilty
if it isn't feasible for your family.

The sick person
may become confused, disoriented, and
need medical and psychological care
not available
outside of a hospital facility.

When a loved one is ill,
family members may be torn
between responsibility for the sick person
and for
the other members of the household.

The unity of the home is disrupted
when the members
can *no longer* accept the added tension
of a crisis situation
and feelings, formerly controlled,
explode.

Pressures—physical, emotional, and social—
may be unbearable,
particularly if the illness
is a lingering one.

Frustration and fatigue
can deplete the strength
of the most loving and devoted person.

Weigh all the choices.
Take time to decide.
Seek support of professionals, friends, and other
family members, including
the sick person—
if you can.

Hospitals and Nursing Homes

When home care is not feasible,
hospitals and nursing homes
may be appropriate places for your loved one.

Check carefully the reputation,
facilities, and personnel of
any hospital or nursing home
you consider.

Look for

—smaller, specialized wards,
offering individualized treatment.

—Even in a large facility,
you can find intimacy and
warmth.

—Surround your loved one with
familiar things
that he or she values.

—Decorate the room with personal items.
Arrange to bring in favorite foods occasionally.

—See if your beloved
could conveniently wear his or her own
nightclothes
rather than the usual hospital garb.

Throughout the country,
families and friends
are challenging the
once sacred
institutional rules, regulations, and
visiting policies that
isolate them
from their loved one.

Long-established rules
are being revised.

Small children may be allowed to
visit the sick person.

Visiting hours have become more flexible.

Patients and their families
may participate in the planning and
carrying out of care.

As closely as possible, attempt
to provide
the kind of loving care
that you would give
at home.

Don't be surprised if your
requests are denied—and don't
give up.

Be persistent.

Speak to the administrator, if necessary,
to get an adequate reason
for the refusal—or a
reversal of policy.

The Hospice Idea

Since 1967, another setting
has been available for the dying person.

Historically, a hospice
was both hospital and hotel.
Pilgrims could stop there
for rest and sustenance.

Today, the hospice
is a place for respite
but not cure.

In St. Christopher's in England
the wards are noted for
their spaciousness and peaceful atmosphere.
Big windows, fill the hospice with light.
There are flowers everywhere.

Visitors come
whenever they like,
stay as long as they want
but never on Monday—
Monday is "relatives' day off."
The hairdresser comes,
and the hospice holds parties and concerts.

In the dining room
patients, visitors, staff and their children
(yes, there is a daycare center at the hospice)
gather for meals.

Patients are allowed to make decisions,
read when they want,
eat in the garden at their leisure,
keep their own clothes,
bring a familiar chair from home.

The hospice staff extends home visiting
with an outpatient team of
cooperative physicians, nurses, clergy, and
social workers.

The patients' final days
are relatively free of pain.
No heroic resuscitations
are undertaken.
There is a skillful tailoring
of medication
to individual needs.

No wonder then
that hundreds of hospices
with varying approaches—
some for children only,
some with home care and some in hospitals—
are springing up all over America.

They can create a warm, accommodating
atmosphere
for family and friends
to say a loving good-bye.

The hospice is an idea
whose time has come.

6

HELPING YOURSELF

If I am not for myself,
who will be for me?

—HILLEL

107•

Caring for a person in poor health
is a demanding responsibility.

You just cannot devote
every minute
of every day
to vigilant watchfulness
over your loved one.

You need time . . .

To Relax Emotionally

In times of stress,
it is important that
you continue to live your life
as normally as possible.

You need interludes of emotional,
physical, and spiritual rest,
some space for

respite,
reprieve, and
re-creation.

Try to find a quiet time for yourself
each day,
even "five-minute vacations."
Wind down and try to relax.

There is healing in solitude.

A little withdrawal from
the constant tension
allows you to return to your beloved
refreshed, renewed, restored—

a little different
from the distraught person you were.

Alcohol and drugs may seem to be
the instant relaxation you need
to ease your fears and anxieties.

Wait.

You are only smothering
your pain artificially.

Drugs have built-in dangers.

They may:
Delay your grief.
Deepen your depression.
Become addictive.

Sedation is no cure
for grief.

Overbusyness can lure
you away
from facing your pain.

There are dangers.
When activities reach a frenzied pitch,
the body gives way to exhaustion.

You need time . . .

To Relax Physically

More than ever
you should try to stay healthy.

Do not skip meals.
Proper nutrition is vital.

Regular exercise releases pent-up feelings
and keeps your body strong.
Sufficient sleep fights physical fatigue.

You must maintain your health
if you are to take care of
your beloved effectively.

Just as important as it is for you
to be alone,
so you
need time . . .

To Share with Friends

"I have so much on my mind.
Just doing those things that need to be done
consumes my every moment.
I can't think of being with anyone else."

Yes, you are tired and weary.
But you need other people
like never before.

Don't escape into loneliness.

Share with trusted friends
your thoughts and fears.

Choose carefully those friends
who will accept and understand,
who will not fault you
or deny your feelings.

Emotions that are denied expression
grow in isolation.

People need people
and friends need friends
because we *all* need love.

Don't "lock up your hearts"
and fail to heed
the outstretched hand of
a kindred spirit,
willing to share your burdens.

As you relax physically and
emotionally
consider also
a time . . .

To Relax Spiritually

Perhaps more than any other event
the loss of health
raises the most urgent issues
about

good and evil,
reward and punishment,
of why terrible things happen to a loved one.

Your religion may provide you
with a spiritual philosophy
that helps you make some sense of
sickness and health.

Beware.

Religion can be hazardous to your health,
when you believe you haven't prayed hard
enough,
and punishment is linked with illness.

Religion then becomes a tool
for denial of real emotions and
keeps you from releasing feelings of
helplessness, guilt, anger.

A mature, forgiving, open faith
encourages expression,
allows your angry cry to heaven—
    "How could you, God!"

Religion offers no absolute answers,
no guarantee of special treatment,
no extended length of time for your beloved.

For many,
faith *does*

help its believers
to accept the unacceptable,
and to ennoble
ignoble misfortune.

7

HELPING
YOUR
LOVED
ONE

"He needs me.
I need him.
We need each other."

—WORDS OF PATIENT AND FAMILY

A Time to Visit

Illness is one task that
each person must perform
entirely by himself or herself.

That is not to say
that your loved one
should be *alone*.

Visit frequently,
if your loved one is not at home.

Share news of the family.

Seek your beloved's advice,
so he or she will know that
his or her judgment *still* is valued.

Bring small gifts.

Especially bring yourself.

You may find it painful
visiting an ailing person,
especially someone with an advanced disease.

When a loved one's features
change markedly,
it is hard to believe
you are with the same person.

It is difficult to keep eye contact.
Words don't come easily.

You try to act naturally,
but you feel awkward.

Suddenly, your beloved
seems a stranger.

Think of the person
you knew.
Inside he or she is probably
the same.

"Real isn't how you are made," said the Skin Horse.
"It's a thing that happens to you."
"Does it hurt?" asked the Rabbit.
"Sometimes," said the Skin Horse, for he was always
truthful.
"When you are Real, you don't mind being hurt. It doesn't
often happen to people who break easily, or have sharp
edges, or who have to be carefully kept. Generally, by the
time you are Real, most of your hair has been loved off, and
your eyes drop out, and you get loose in the joints and very
shabby. But these things don't matter at all, because once
you are Real, you can't be ugly, except to people who don't
understand."

—MARGARITE WILLIAMS
THE VELVETEEN RABBIT

A Time to Talk

Not with—
   "Snap out of it.
     Everything will be fine, you'll see.
     Try to get hold of yourself."
Chattering isn't communication.

Neither is denial.

Your loved one doesn't need
platitudes and reassurances
that you both
know are false.

They signal your beloved
not to share, but
to hide
real fear and feelings
from you.

Don't try to make life "normal"
by pretending nothing is wrong.

At the same time
avoid saying
"terminal" or "hopeless."

Such words make the dying person feel
written off
the rolls of the living.

Stress
that you and the doctors
will do all you can
to make your loved one's life as happy and as
comfortable as possible.

Look your loved one in the eye.
Be open and straightforward.

You allow an
honest exchange of feelings
when you say:
    "It must be hard for you, isn't it?
    I'd like to help you, but I
    don't know what to do—
    what would you suggest?"

Don't be afraid of admitting
    your anxiety,
    your indecision, and
    your pain.

Even though no one
can truly understand
another person's feelings,
try to empathize and
identify with your loved one's feelings.

Ask yourself:
  "Knowing my beloved as I do,
    how would I react
    if it were I?"

The person may feel a need
to talk not only about the illness
but about
the happy moments of his or her life.

A loved one needs to know
that his or her life on earth
does have an impact upon others.

Consider:
a tape recording of the life for an oral history
to be *forever* chronicled.

Or an album of pictures
and of keepsakes.

These records of one's life
reduce feelings of
meaninglessness and absurdity.

A Time to Listen

During moments of crisis,
many people are so concerned
about *what* to say,
that they frame answers
without hearing what is said.

More important than your words
is your ability to listen
not only to what is said,
but to how it is said
and what is meant, and

to seize the secret messages of silence.

Listen between the lines—
emotional content, body language,
silences, avoided topics.

Eyes averted,
turned-down head,
posture-shifts,
the tone of voice

may speak louder than words.

Allow full expression of
fears and nightmares.
   "Will there be severe pain?
   Will I suffocate?
   Will I be all hooked up to beeping monitors?"

Tell your loved one:
   "It is normal to express these fears.
   I'm glad you shared your thoughts with me.
   Didn't the doctor assure you that . . ."

Serious illness may be a time
when courage runs quite thin and faith
is but a theological abstraction.

Have the courage to listen to things
that are not always pleasant to hear.

Sometimes, all that is needed
is your being there,

and saying nothing.

Rather than a forced conversation,
the best communication
may be a thoughtful silence, and
a tender touch.

A patient said:
  "The person who helped me the most
  said very little.
  But I knew by his look and his manner
  that he knew what I was experiencing.
  There was an 'I know' meeting of
  two hearts, especially
  when I saw tears glisten in his eyes."

A Time to Cry

Tears are wordless messages,
a vital part of grieving.

Pain can be eased
when people are able
to weep together.

Friends and family
may believe that
crying *in front of*
or *with* a sick person
will be upsetting to the loved one.

Not true.

An ill child said to her parents:
   "Aren't you sad that I'm so sick?
    Don't you care?
    How come I've never seen you cry?"

A Time to Touch

Sickness can make a person
feel very lonely and apart.

An ill person needs more than ever
to be close to the living.

The sense of touch
reduces the bleakest of all feelings—
abandonment.

Holding your loved one communicates:
"No matter how serious the illness,
feelings toward me have not changed:
   I am not rejected.
   I am not untouchable."

Don't be afraid to reach out physically:
a warm embrace,
a firm handshake, a pat on the shoulder,
the gentle stroking of the forehead,
a soothing and comforting massage . . .

When words fail,
the touch of reassurance is vital.

Hugging, holding, kissing
may be the best medicine
for your loved one
and for you.

They say:

"I love you."

A Time to Laugh

Sick people especially need
lightness and smiles in their lives.

People who have a good sense of humor
often maintain their sense of humor
in their illness.

Somberness
won't make you or your loved one better.

A sick person quipped:
    "My situation is hopeless
        but not serious."

Humor helped her manage feelings
that were too great to deal with openly.

The threat of her future
was no less menacing,
but it became easier to bear.

Laughing together
is one of the normal ways
that people relate to each other.

One patient said to a chaplain:

"You've become so morbid and gloomy
   since you heard my prognosis.
   You used to tell me such funny
   stories.
   I'm the same person that I was
   before the diagnosis.
   How come you aren't fun anymore?"

8

HELPING
EACH
OTHER

*"Friends keep asking
me why I'm a hospice
volunteer. Frankly I
get more out of it
than I give."*

The fact that one person is seriously ill
doesn't mean
that another person's heart should stop loving.

Would you trade in
your life's experiences with your beloved
because of all
the pain and anguish you are having now?

Your love can now
grow,
knowing the limits of time, or
diminish
because of the pain of illness.

This is your real choice in anticipating grief—
to *grow* or
to *diminish*.

"All persons are mortal.
I am a person.
Therefore, I am mortal.
(But I don't believe it.)"

Now you are *beginning*
to realize that good health may
not always be permanent.

The slogan
"Today is the first day
of the rest of your life"
is but a half-truth.

Now you know the other half.

"Today may also be the last day
you'll ever get."

No one knows about tomorrow.

In short, when you actually
become aware of the fragility of life,
you will see your life differently.

There is a noticeable shift in your priorities,
an intensive soul-searching for new meanings,
and the use of your energy for
what is really important.

You realize that the two *least*
important details
are usually inscribed upon the tombstone—
dates of birth and death.

You will not be remembered
for the *length* of your years, but for
 the *breadth* of your sympathies for others,
 the *depth* of your appreciation for beauty,
 the *height* of your love.

Through this personal transformation,
you experience an opportunity for growth
by *shedding* those attitudes
that prevent you
from living life—
strengthening those qualities
that add depth to your being.

As you work through your loved one's sickness
you become aware
of the treasures
that comprise life.

The big things in life
suddenly become small,
the small things
very large.

You are setting new priorities.
Sometimes the simple things of life
become the most enjoyable.

You may not be afraid of
crippling illness
but of the incompleteness of life.

Yet, even with serious illness,
there may yet be golden days you will never
forget.

Love has no rigid bounds.
Love goes beyond the self,
beyond a precious loved one,
flowing freely,
reaching out,
touching, as it flows.

Love is hard,
but
it makes everything else easier.

In the midst of sickness
your loved one is helping you
to confront life,
finding

comfort in your crisis, and
acceptance in your anguish.

A final thought:

A little boy confused his prayer,
saying:

> "Now I lay me down to sleep,
> I pray the Lord my soul to keep,
> if I should die
> before I . . .
> *live.*"

The real tragedy is
to *die*
before you *live.*

One woman said—

"Having to face the fact
that my husband is so ill
makes us value our love
with an intensity and intimacy
that we had never known before.
Each day becomes a gift
to experience together.
No longer do we take our
relationship for *granted*."

As you discover so much
about your beloved—
the hurts, fears, hopes—

so are you learning
so much about yourself.

Each day is another day of life
to be enjoyed together
as fully as you can.

*"What we have once enjoyed
we can never lose.
All that we love deeply
becomes a part of us."*
—HELEN KELLER

To Every Thing There Is a Season

*To every thing there is a season, and a time
to every purpose under the heaven;*

*a time to be born, and a time to die,
a time to plant, and a time to pluck up
that which is planted;*

*a time to kill, and a time to heal;
a time to break down, and a time to build up;*

*a time to weep, and a time to laugh;
a time to mourn, and a time to dance;*

*a time to cast away stones, and a time
to gather stones together; a time to embrace,
and a time to refrain from embracing;*

*a time to get, and a time to lose;
a time to keep, and a time to cast away;*

*a time to rend, and a time to sew;
a time to keep silence, and a time to speak;*

*a time to love, and a time to hate;
a time of war, and a time of peace.*

—Ecclesiastes 3:1–8

ॐ 9

DECISIONS
NEAR
THE END
OF LIFE

"I could keep this patient alive. But why?"

—A PHYSICIAN WHOSE PATIENT IS
STRUGGLING WITH TERMINAL ILLNESS

Technological advances make it possible to prolong the lives of those who, decades ago, would not have survived an illness.

Thankfully, countless lives are being saved; individuals who once would have been given a death sentence now have the opportunity to participate in the lives of their families and friends.

There is a flip side, however.

Consider dying or comatose patients hooked up—
sometimes painfully—to a life support machine
with no true hope for recovery.

We may extend the length of life, but not always
the quality of life.

Most dying patients want the right to choose whether or not to accept intrusive procedures that only marginally lengthen their lives.

Pope Pius XII said that it is permissible to use, with moderation, narcotics that will allay suffering but also cause a quicker death.

The pope added that he did not consider the use of respirators obligatory, "since this form of treatment goes beyond ordinary methods."

A signed "living will" (or "directive to physicians" or "treatment directives") can become the voice of the terminally ill person who is unable to communicate.

These documents allow patients the right to choose—to determine their future medical treatment.

A living will promotes patient autonomy and relieves family or friends of the onerous decision of when to stop or continue treatment.

The appointment of a durable power of attorney allows an agent to interpret instructions when the patient becomes unable to communicate.

The United States Supreme Court has affirmed the legality of the living will. (See *Where to Go for Help: Choice in Dying.*)

Patients have taught us that dying involves the whole person—not only the physical body, but emotional and spiritual aspects as well.

Just as people can choose to live with integrity, they also have the right to choose to die with dignity.

APPENDIX

A Decalogue for Helping the Seriously Ill for Those Who Care for Them

THOU SHALT NOT

I. Be Afraid to Touch
Touching is one of the most comforting modes of communication. A squeeze of the hand or a warm embrace eloquently testifies to how much you truly care.

II. Hesitate to Smile and Laugh
Not with forced frivolity but with the sheer enjoyment of humorous incidents and stories. Serious illness does not put a ban on laughter.

III. Be Uncomfortable with Silence
Love understands love; it needs no words. Silence can be as supportive as shared conversation.

IV. Offer Untrue Statements
When a patient may be doing poorly, don't say:

"You're doing so well."
"There's nothing seriously wrong."
"You'll soon be as good as new."

Everyone—the sick and healthy—should be treated with dignity and not deceit.

V. Believe You Need to Have All the Answers and Solve All the Problems
Just listen and hear what is said. There are times when there are no complete solutions. Accept your own limited self and commit yourself only to what you are able to do.

THOU SHALT

VI. Accept the Feelings of the Sick Person
Don't pretend that everything is OK. A seriously ill person needs to express his or her emotions. You can encourage that individual by saying: "What are you feeling?" "Tell me what's happening to you." "It must be very hard."
Be sensitive to shifting feelings, whether they be sadness, rage, panic, or frustration.

VII. Share Time Together
Talking, listening to music, watching television, playing cards or games can help fill lonely and frightening hours with shared companionship.

VIII. Offer to Help
"I'm going to the supermarket. Can I pick up something for you?"
"I'll take your kids to the school picnic."
"While the nurse is away this afternoon, I'll come over to the house."
Actions do often speak louder than words.

IX. Locate Other Supports
There may be many people and organizations who can offer invaluable assistance—family, friends, church/synagogue, home health care, self-help groups, medical organizations. These vital people and groups can help to better manage the difficult moments for both patient and significant other.

X. Respect the Privacy and Integrity of the Sick Person
If possible, call before you visit. You might inquire: "Do you feel like company this morning?" Never assume you know what the person's needs may be at any given moment. And always, always keep knowledge of the patient confidential.

Communication between Patient, Family, and Medical Staff

*When speaking with physician
or medical personnel*

—Write down questions in advance. Thoughts should be expressed clearly and kept to a reasonable limit.
—Communicate honestly about the concerns and fears of both patient and family members.
—Give accurate medical information.
—Respect the medical staff's time and expect the same in return.
—Cooperate fully once a decision on treatment has been mutually agreed upon.

*Questions to ask about the medical
problem/pain/symptom(s)*

—Approximately when did the problem/pain/symptom begin?
—Where?
—How long did the pain last?
—Is pain constant or changeable?
—Located in one area or other parts of the body?
—What makes it worse?
—What helps the patient to feel better?

—On a scale of 1 to 10, with 10 being the worst, how would the pain be measured?
—Other questions?

Questions to ask about the diagnosis

—Medical name of illness?
—Possible cause?
—How to prevent the illness from worsening?
—Projected tests, treatments, medications? (See below.)
—Need for another medical opinion?
—Prognosis?
—Other questions?

Questions to ask about possible tests

Patients who are generally aware of the effects of tests and treatment are usually less apprehensive and recover more rapidly.
—Suggested test(s)?
—Purpose?
—How administered?
—Risks?
—Side-effects?
—Can patient have someone accompany him/her during the tests?
—Can patient return home/to work after test?
—Possible medical consequences if patient refuses the test?
—Alternatives to these prescribed tests?
—When will results be known?
—Fees? (Covered by insurance?)
—Other questions?

Questions to ask about possible treatment

Consent should be based on a reasonable understanding of the nature of the treatment and risks involved.
—Suggested treatment?
—Purpose?
—How administered?
—Expected length of treatment?
—Risks?
—Side-effects?
—Another medical opinion?
—Possible medical consequences if patient refuses treatment?
—Alternative treatments?
—How to evaluate success or failure of treatment?
—Fees? (Covered by insurance?)
—Other questions?

Questions to ask about pain control

Effective pain control is giving the patient the right medicine in the right amount in the right way at the right time. Proper pain medication helps to prevent pain from returning while keeping the sick person as alert as possible.
—Name of medicine(s) or drug(s)?
—Purpose?
—Special instructions?
—Frequency?
—Risks?
—Are other physicians involved in treatment aware of the dispensation of these special medications?
—Foods, liquids, activities to be avoided while taking these drugs?

—Side effects?
—How to evaluate success or failure of medicines?
—Can prescription be refilled?
—Expenses? (Covered by medical insurance? Other generic equivalents?)
—Other questions?

Prescription Drug Record

Date	Drug	Dosage	Physician	Results

Questions to ask about the physician

—Training?
—Specialization?
—Reputation?
—Hospital affiliation?
—Flexibility?
—Ability to relate to patient and family?
—Fees? (Covered by medical insurance?)
—Availability for consultation with other medical personnel?
—Other questions?

Vital Information Concerning the Seriously Ill Person

1. Full and legal name: _____

   Previous surname if applicable: _____

2. Legal residence: _____

   Town/city: _____

   Telephone number: _____

3. Date of birth: _____ Place of birth: _____

4. Marital status (circle answer)

   single   married   widowed   divorced

5. Language spoken: _____

6. Social security number: _____

7. Primary physician: _____

   Telephone number: _____

8. Other specialists: _____

   Telephone number: _____

   _____ Telephone number: _____

   _____ Telephone number: _____

9. Hospital or health care facility: _____

_____

10. Medical insurance policies, type, policy, and where
    kept: _____

_____

11. Nurse and/or visiting nursing association: _____

_____

12. Blood type, Rh factor: _____

13. Allergies to medication, food: _____

14. Druggist/pharmacy: _____
    Telephone number: _____

_____

15. Dentist: _____
    Telephone number: _____

16. In case of emergency call: _____
    Telephone number: _____

_____

_____

17. Clergyperson: _____
    Telephone number: _____

18. Self-help group: _____

Telephone number: _____

_____

19. Taxi or transportation: _____

    Telephone number: _____

20. Helpful organizations: _____

    Telephone number: _____

    _____Telephone number: _____

    _____Telephone number: _____

21. Full name of father: _____

    Birthplace and residence if living: _____

22. Full name of mother (including maiden name):

    _____

    Birthplace and residence if living: _____

23. Names of surviving brother(s): _____

    Address: _____

    _____ Address: _____

    _____ Address: _____

24. Names of surviving sister(s): _____

    Address: _____

    _____ Address: _____

    _____ Address: _____

25. Names of surviving son(s): _____

    Address: _____

    _____ Address: _____

    _____ Address: _____

26. Names of surviving daughter(s): _____

    Address: _____

    _____ Address: _____

    _____ Address: _____

27. Names of grandchildren/great-grandchildren:

    _____

    Address: _____

    _____ Address: _____

    _____ Address: _____

    _____ Address: _____

28. Names of close friends: _____

    _____ Address: _____

    _____ Address: _____

    _____ Address: _____

29. If married, full name of spouse (maiden name also):

    _____

    _____

If widowed, full name of spouse and place of death:

_____

_____

If divorced, full name of former spouse: _____

_____

30. Attorney: _____

    Telephone number: _____

31. Accountant/financial advisor(s): _____

    Telephone number(s): _____

32. Executor of estate: _____

    Telephone number: _____

33. Location of will: _____

_____

34. Safety deposit box(es): _____

    Location: _____ Box number(s): _____

    Key number: _____

35. Other important papers and policies and where

    kept: _____

_____

_____

_____

36. If a veteran of United States armed services, service serial number: _____

_____

Veterans Administration "C" number: _____

37. In case of death:

Funeral home: _____

Address: _____

Telephone number: _____

If funeral arrangements are prearranged, location and policy number: _____

_____

Other arrangements: _____

_____

_____

_____

38. Internment plot number: _____

At: _____

Owner of cemetery plot: _____

Relationship to owner: _____

If plot is not purchased, suggest: _____

_____

Other arrangements: _____

_____

39. Local hospice, if needed: _____

    Telephone number: _____

40. Organizational   Offices held:
    affiliations:

_____   _____

_____   _____

_____   _____

41. List any special thoughts or requests: _____

_____

_____

_____

_____

_____

_____

_____

_____

_____

_____

Where to Go for Help

Mark Twain said, "It's not what people know that gets them into trouble, but it's what they know that isn't so." Many organizations can help you work through your questions, fears, and frustrations. The resources listed below provide important information about serious illness and support systems to assist you in coping.

If you need help immediately, contact the social service department of your hospital. These professionals will assist you with problem-solving, counseling services, and information about community, regional, and national organizations.

AIDS

What is AIDS?

Acquired Immune Deficiency Syndrome breaks down the body's immune system, destroying the body's ability to fight infection and illness. AIDS is caused by the Human Immunodeficiency Virus (HIV). By preventing HIV infection, we can prevent AIDS. Having HIV does not mean a person has AIDS; persons with HIV may or may not develop AIDS. The World Health Organization notes that in 1993, 12 million people were infected with HIV, including 1.5 million in the United States.

How does one get HIV?

—By having sex (heterosexual or homosexual) with someone who has HIV;

—By sharing drug needles or syringes with a person who has the HIV virus;

—By contact with infected blood or blood products (since 1984 tests used to screen blood and blood products make the risk of HIV infection from these sources very low);

—By transmission of the virus from a mother to her baby during pregnancy.

Is there a cure for AIDS?

At this time, there is no cure for AIDS, but researchers are working on an AIDS vaccine. Three drugs have been approved by the U.S. Food and Drug Administration to treat persons with AIDS: AZT, ddi, and ddc. There is much experimentation in AIDS treatment and cure taking place throughout the world.

Myths about AIDS

Myth: AIDS can be transmitted by casual contact. **Fact:** No case of AIDS has been caused by touching, hugging, or living with a person with AIDS. HIV is not transmitted by shaking hands with or breathing the same air as an infected person, even in close quarters like a crowded train, classroom, or office.

Myth: You can get AIDS from using public water fountains, swimming pools, toilets, telephones, and laundries. **Fact:** The HIV virus is very fragile and does not survive long outside the human body. Since it is not spread through air, food, or water, touching something someone with AIDS has touched cannot give you AIDS.

Myth: You can get AIDS by donating blood. **Fact:** Blood banks use sterile needles that are never used twice.

Myth: Recipients of blood transfusions are at great risk for AIDS. **Fact:** Screening procedures now help identify and eliminate HIV-infected blood.

Myth: Only homosexuals and intravenous drug users are at risk for AIDS. **Fact:** Anyone exposed to HIV in a way that may permit the virus to enter the bloodstream is at risk for AIDS.

Discrimination against AIDS patients

Few diseases in modern times have raised such fears and uncertainties as AIDS. Not only do people with AIDS face the trauma of terminal illness, they are also subjected to inhumane discrimination and isolation. Many are evicted from their homes, lose their jobs, and are denied access to public accommodation and community services. There are school protests against the attendance of children with AIDS. Even though there is *no* evidence of airborne spread of the virus or of spread through casual interpersonal contact, some people still have a pathological dread of any contact whatsoever with AIDS patients.

The psychological impact of an AIDS diagnosis is similar in some respects to that produced by other fatal diseases, but because of the social stigma, psychological reactions to AIDS are compounded. Unlike cancer, which can elicit sympathy, AIDS often provokes shame. One AIDS patient recalls that his father's first reponse upon hearing his son had AIDS was, "You should be ashamed of yourself." There may be even greater denial in AIDS than in other terminal illnesses. There are some AIDS patients whose disbelief is so strong that they refuse medical care. Understandably, AIDS patients often experience episodes of anger and depression. Anger surfaces because many people with the illness are relatively young. Approximately ninety percent of adults with this syndrome are between the ages of twenty and forty-nine. Death is difficult to face at any age, but a premature death is especially unfair. People with AIDS face depression not only because of possible loss of life, but from the possible loss of friends, family, and a supportive social network as well. People with AIDS may also encounter physical and mental limitations—gradual deterioration of mental faculties over a period of months, and perhaps loss of the ability to accomplish simple tasks.

The need for warmth and affection

One person with AIDS remarked, "The challenge is not dying of AIDS but living with AIDS." Other people's fear of contagion may deny those with AIDS the closeness and tenderness that are so vital to all of us. How people contract AIDS is unimportant; what is important is that they now have the disease and need love and support. Listen, share a meal, extend a comforting hand. Being seriously ill doesn't mean being untouchable.

The need for education

Fear is generated by ignorance. Only education can halt the growing fear and unwarranted discrimination against adults and children with AIDS or those suspected of being at risk. We should call upon governmental bodies (legislative, executive, and judicial) to prohibit discrimination against AIDS patients in housing, employment, and health and community services. We should support oral and written education about AIDS, provided by knowledgeable professionals. We must ensure that people with AIDS do not become strangers in their own land.

The need for counseling and support

Counseling can help AIDS patients through their turbulent times. There are AIDS crisis centers and other community agencies for AIDS patients and their families and friends. In addition to psychological support, they may be able to provide legal and financial counseling.

In the United States, contact:

AIDS Clinical Trials Information Service
P.O. Box 6421
Rockville, Maryland 20849

American Red Cross
AIDS Public Education Program
(Contact your local chapter for information)

American Social Health Organization
P.O. Box 13827
Research Triangle Park, North Carolina 27709

Centers for Disease Control
Sexually Transmitted Diseases Division
1600 Clifton Road, NE
Atlanta, Georgia 30333

National AIDS Clearinghouse
1600 Research Boulevard
Rockville, Maryland 20850
(800) 458-5231

National Minority AIDS Council
300 I Street, NE, Suite 400
Washington, D.C. 20002
(202) 544-1076

Pediatric AIDS Foundation
1311 Colorado Avenue
Santa Monica, California 90404
(800) 488-5000

Hotlines
Gay/Lesbian Youth
(800) 347-TEEN

National Institute of Drug Abuse (NIDA)
(800) 662-HELP

National Sexually Transmitted Disease
(800) 227-8922

In Canada, contact:
Canadian AIDS Society
400–100 Sparks Street
Ottawa, Ontario K1P 5BZ

National AIDS Secretariat
Jeanne Marise Building
Room 1742
Ottawa, Ontario K1A 0K9

Canadian Hemophilia Society
National Office 1450
Rue City Councillors
Bureau 840
Montreal, Quebec H3A 2E6

Alzheimer's Disease

Approximately one-half of elderly men and women with severe intellectual impairment are victims of Alzheimer's disease. Before a diagnosis can be validated, other illnesses that may cause memory loss must be excluded. Understandably, the person afflicted with Alzheimer's disease finds it difficult to comprehend the changes taking place in his or her thinking and behavior. Caregivers will have questions about the activities the afflicted person may safely engage in and how much encouragement should be given to carry out a familiar activity that becomes painfully frustrating. Through support groups, family members can benefit by sharing experiences with other families facing similar problems.

Contact:

Alzheimer Association
919 North Michigan Avenue
Suite 1000
Chicago, Illinois 60611
(800) 621-0379

Alzheimer's Society of Canada
1320 Yonge Street
Suite 302
Toronto, Ontario M4T 1X2

Arthritis

There are well over 100 different types of arthritis. The three most common are osteoarthritis, fibromyalgia, and rheumatoid arthritis. Many forms are painful and sometimes debilitating, and some, such as lupus and scleroderma, can be fatal. Causes and treatments can vary greatly between different kinds of arthritis. Your physician will describe the various forms of treatment and projected results.

Contact:

The Arthritis Foundation
1314 Spring Street, NW
Atlanta, Georgia 30309
(800) 283-7800

The Arthritis Society of Canada
250 Bloor Street, East
Suite 401
Toronto, Ontario M4W 3PC

Blood Collections and Donations

Since 1881, people have turned to the American Red Cross for emergency services. Today, 1.4 million trained and dedicated American Red Cross volunteers help their neighbors daily. Each year, they collect more than 6 million units of blood from more than 4 million blood volunteers. These donations amount to nearly half the nation's blood supply and save countless lives.

Red Cross services include:

—Offering patients the opportunity to donate their own blood for certain kinds of surgery.
—Identifying and recruiting healthy blood donors to help ensure an adequate blood supply.
—Educating physicians and patients about blood and the latest techniques in blood transfusions.
—Conducting research to help improve the safety and therapeutic benefits of blood.
—Maintaining a national registry of thousands of volunteer donors who provide rare blood types to meet emergency needs.

—Lending technical assistance to hospitals, their blood banks, and medical staffs.

Contact your local chapter of the American or Canadian Red Cross or:

American National Red Cross
17th and D Steets, NW
Washington, D.C. 20006

Canadian Red Cross Society
1800 Alta Vista Drive
Ottawa, Ontario K1G 4J5

Cancer

In 1913, when the American Cancer Society first opened its doors, the word *cancer* was rarely printed in magazines or newspapers or spoken aloud. Cancer patients felt isolated and doomed. Cancer research held little interest or promise for most scientists and physicians. No one spoke of a "cure rate"—the disease was assumed to be fatal.

Today, these attitudes and situations have almost completely changed. It is now recognized that many cancers can be cured if detected and treated promptly and properly. Today, the cancer survival rate in the United States is 51 percent. With present knowledge and treatments, it is possible to save at least 55 percent of all patients—as experience in leading cancer centers shows. These facts have revolutionized public and professional attitudes; today in the United States, people everywhere are joining in the fight against cancer, and this has helped save lives.

The American Cancer Society is a nationwide,

community-based, voluntary health organization dedicated to eliminating cancer as a major health problem by prevention, saving lives, and diminishing suffering from cancer. It is one of the oldest and largest voluntary health agencies in the United States, with over two million Americans united to conquer cancer through balanced programs of research, education, patient service, and rehabilitation. The American Cancer Society, Inc., consists of a National Society, 57 chartered divisions, and more than 3,000 local units.

The American Cancer Society provides services for cancer patients, including information and referral, and transportation and nursing services (on a limited basis depending upon the resources of the county unit). Hospital equipment is often loaned to patients who wish to go home but require special facilities.

In addition to these general services, the society sponsors trained visitor programs. The Reach to Recovery rehabilitation program is designed to help women who have undergone mastectomy deal with their new physical, psychological, and cosmetic needs. To help new ostomates, the Ostomy Rehabilitation Program trains well-adjusted volunteer ostomates in a course of lectures, films, simulated interviews, and supervised hospital visits. The International Association of Laryngectomees, sponsored by the American Cancer Society, offers psychological support to new laryngectomees and their families. I Can Cope is a group educational program for patients and families to learn from health professionals about such topics as treatment methods, side effects of therapy, approaches to nutrition, and coping skills.

Contact:
American Cancer Society
1599 Clifton Road, NE
Atlanta, Georgia 30329
(800) ACS-2345

Canadian Cancer Society
10 Alcorn Avenue
Suite 200
Toronto, Ontario M4V 3B1

The Cancer Information Service (CIS) is a nationwide network of 19 regional offices supported by the National Cancer Institute (NCI), the U.S. government's primary agency for cancer research. Through its toll-free telephone service, the CIS provides accurate, up-to-date information on cancer to patients and their families, health professionals, and the general public. Through its outreach program, the CIS serves as a resource for state and regional organizations by providing printed materials and technical assistance to cancer education, media campaigns, and community programs. The CIS offices are located at NCI-designated cancer centers and other health care institutions.

Contact:
Cancer Information Service (CIS)
National Cancer Institute
Building 31, Room 10A 24
Bethesda, Maryland 20892
(800) 4-CANCER

Canadian Cancer Institute
755 Concession Street
Hamilton, Ontario L8V 1C4

Cancer Research Society
Box 183
19 Esterel, Place Bonadventure
Montreal, Quebec H5A 1A9

Leukemia is an acute or chronic disease characterized by an abnormal increase in the number of leukocytes (any of the white or colorless nucleated cells that occur in the blood). Although often thought of as a childhood disease, leukemia strikes many more adults than children; for example, in 1994 there were an estimated 26,000 incidents of leukemia in adults and 2,600 in children. The five-year survival rate is 38 percent. The 57 chapters of the Leukemia Society of America provide education, professional consultation, referral service, research programs, and family support for patients and families. (See also Children with Cancer.)

Contact:

The Leukemia Society of America
600 Third Avenue
New York, New York 10016

The Leukemia Society of Canada
750 Marcel Laurin
Suite B60
Ville-St. Laurent, Quebec H4M 2M4

An ostomy is an operation such as a colostomy that creates an artificial passage for elimination of bodily wastes. The United Ostomy Association was founded for understanding and support. Five hundred and ninety-four chapters throughout the United States and Canada provide important informational materials, visits to support new patients, transportation to physicians, and support groups.

Contact:
United Ostomy Association
36 Executive Park
Suite 120
Irvine, California 92714

Centers for Grieving Children

There are support groups for children who may be experiencing the death of a loved one. Programs such as The Centre for Living with Dying in Santa Clara, California; the Good Grief Program in Boston, Massachusetts; The Dougy Center in Portland, Oregon; Fernside in Cincinnati, Ohio; and Kids Grieve Too in Seattle, Washington, offer important resources. For a Directory of Children's Support Programs with geographic locations, age ranges, and professional staff,

Contact:
The Dougy Center
3909 SE 52d Avenue
Portland, Oregon 97286

Children's Hospice

Hospice care for children incorporates both a philosophy of caring and a system of comprehensive, interdisciplinary services for children and adolescents with life-threatening conditions, and for those family members or significant others who provide the child's immediate support.

Hospice care for children aims to enhance the quality of life for the child and family as they define it. It includes the child and family in the decision-making process about services and treatment to the fullest degree possible. It addresses the physical, developmental, psychological, social, and spiritual needs of children and families through individualized plans of care. It ensures continuity and consistency of care in all settings where services are provided.

Hospice provides coordinated care—outpatient, inpatient, and at home—through an interdisciplinary team coordinated by a qualified physician and registered nurse. Hospice care is also attentive to needs related to loss and grieving for all concerned prior to and following a death. Nursing services are available twenty-four hours a day in any setting in which care is provided. Services are systematically evaluated for appropriateness and effectiveness.

The interdisciplinary service team is supported through educational and professional training programs that enhance skills, and through appropriate individual and group activities.

Contact:

Children's Hospice International
901 North Washington Street
Alexandria, Virginia 22314
(800) 2-4-CHILD

Children's Hospitalization

When family members bring a child with a life-threatening illness to a hospital in another city, they need psychological support and affordable housing.

Communities around the world have banded together to create "homes away from home," known as Ronald McDonald Houses, for families with seriously ill children being treated at local hospitals. In so doing, they have realized the benefits of working together toward a common goal, as well as that special feeling that comes from helping others in times of need. The people in these communities have established more than 158 Ronald McDonald Houses in eleven countries, each of which operates as a separate not-for-profit organization. Among those who donate their time and resources to each House are members of the area's medical community, local parent volunteers, and McDonald's owner/operators and their employees and families. Their combined efforts have created Houses that are overnight "homes" to more than 4,000 family members of sick children. And in turn, each night the residents of Ronald McDonald Houses support one another with the comfort and care that can only be given by people who find themselves in similar situations.

Contact:
Ronald McDonald House
500 North Michigan Avenue
Suite 200
Chicago, Illinois 60611

Hospital for Sick Children Foundation
55 University Avenue
Toronto, Ontario M56 1X8

Children's Make-a-Wish

Children with life-threatening illnesses may have hopes and dreams that may never be achieved because of their sickness. Make-a-Wish Foundation is the nation's largest, nonprofit, wish-granting charity, with more than eighty local chapters in the United States and Canada. This organization may provide transportation, meals, lodging, and spending money, and may help include the family in the experience of fulfilling a child's special dream.

Contact:
Make-a-Wish Foundation of America
100 West Clarendon Avenue
Suite 2200
Phoenix, Arizona 85103
(800) 722-9474

For an annual list of other groups granting wishes of children with life-threatening, chronic, or terminal illness,

Contact:
The Candlelighters Childhood Cancer Foundation
7910 Woodmont Avenue
Suite 460
Bethesda, Maryland 20814
(800) 366-2223

The Children's Wish Foundation
1735 Bayly Street
Suite 8C
Pickering, Ontario L1W 3G7

Children with Cancer

Cancer is the number-one cause of death by disease in children. By the year 2000, one in every 900 adults will be a survivor of childhood cancer. This growing population has unique issues and needs.

The Candlelighters Childhood Cancer Foundation is an international organization of parents of children with cancer, survivors of childhood cancer, and interested professionals. Formed in 1970, it has over 400 groups with more than 40,000 members in every state in the United States and on every continent. A statement from a Candlelighters publication summarizes the organization's focus: "Candlelighters parents share the shock of diagnosis, the questions about treatment, the anxiety of waiting, the despair of relapse, the grief of death, the despondency of loss, the hope of remission, the joy of cure."

In addition to local meetings and other planned activities, the national office offers publications and programs to promote concern for and awareness of the problems of childhood cancer and research into its cause and cure. The Candlelighters Survivors of Childhood Cancer Network links long-term survivors with a quarterly newsletter, *The Phoenix*. Their Ombudsman Program helps families and survivors resolve problems in the areas of employment, insurance, and second opinions. Members share information, solve practical problems, and play an informed, active role in the treatment and care of childhood cancer. The Foundation can also provide a list of overnight and day camp programs for children with cancer and their siblings.

Contact:

The Candlelighters Childhood Cancer Foundation
7910 Woodmont Avenue
Suite 460
Bethesda, Maryland 20814
(800) 366-2223

The American Cancer Society can provide information to parents, siblings, teachers, and classmates about the special needs of children with cancer. Information about advances in treating pediatric cancers is also available to health professionals.

Contact:

American Cancer Society
1599 Clifton Road, NE
Atlanta, Georgia 30329
(800) ACS-2345

Canadian Cancer Society
10 Alcorn Avenue
Suite 200
Toronto, Ontario M4V 3B1

Canuck Place, a hospice for children in Canada, is the first free-standing hospice for children in North America. It serves children with progressive life-threatening illnesses and their families through respite, palliative, and bereavement care programs. Opening in early 1995, it provides family-centered care in a homelike environment through its interdisciplinary staff of caregivers, as well as community-based care in conjunction with local health care providers. Its education and research programs contribute to the development of pediatric hospice care.

Contact:

Canuck Place
1690 Mathews Avenue
Vancouver, British Columbia V6J 2T2

Choice in Dying

With the advent of drugs, surgical techniques, and life-sustaining technologies, modern medicine can prolong the lives of seriously ill people. Today, many people want a choice in determining the treatment they are to receive if they become terminally ill.

Choice in Dying is a national, not-for-profit organization working for the rights of patients to make their own medical decisions at the end of life. It provides information about the complex issues of terminal care and the right of patients to control treatment decisions. It will send free, state-specific, *advance directives*—the broad term for "living will" and the durable power of attorney for health care (DPAHC) documents. Choice in Dying has trained legal and educational staff who will answer questions about advance directives and state law free of charge. The group also provides information to families struggling with end-of-life medical treatment decisions. In addition, its legal staff is constantly monitoring legislation, and provides quarterly updates on legislative changes that affect advance directives or end-of-life decision making.

Contact:
Choice in Dying, Inc.
200 Varick Street
New York, New York 10014
(800) 989-WILL

Patients and their families now face difficult decisions about whether to initiate or forgo the use of life-sustaining treatment—choices that did not exist only a

197•

few years ago. The availability of these advanced technologies has also made new and powerful demands on health care providers. Doctors, nurses, hospital administrators, lawyers, social workers, and hospital chaplains are being called upon to participate in a decision-making process that has profound moral implications and is often fraught with uncertainty.

Decisions Near the End of Life deals with some of the toughest issues facing clinicians who care for critically and terminally ill adults. Should caregivers comply with the request of the severely debilitated and depressed AIDS patient who refuses further treatment for his third bout of pneumonia? Can a man in his early sixties with chronic pulmonary disease forgo continued ventilator support because he does not want to live "tethered to a machine"? Should the family of a young woman rendered permanently unconscious by a terrible injury have the right to determine that artificial feeding be terminated? Decisions Near the End of Life is a continuing medical education program developed jointly by Education Development Center, Inc., and The Hastings Center. The program is being distributed by its developers and by the American Hospital Association in collaboration with the American Medical Association and American Bar Association.

Contact:

Education Development Center
"Decisions Near the End of Life"
55 Chapel Street
Newton, Massachusetts 02160

The following is an example of the Choice in Dying *Living Will.* Although all fifty states and the District of

Columbia recognize some form of advance directive (the general term for a living will and a durable power of attorney for health care), laws greatly vary by state. Choice in Dying, a national, not-for-profit organization, recommends that everyone fill out a state-specific advance directive. To obtain a free, state-specific advance directive for your state, call: 1-800-989-WILL (9455) or write to Choice in Dying, 200 Varick Street, 10th Floor, New York, New York 10014-4810.

Living Will

Instructions

Print your name

I, _____,
being of sound mind, make this statement as a directive to be followed if I become permanently unable to participate in decisions regarding my medical care. These instructions reflect my firm and settled commitment to decline medical treatment under the circumstances indicated below:

I direct my attending physician to withhold or withdraw treatment if I should be in an incurable or irreversible mental or physical condition with no reasonable expectation of recovery.

These instructions apply if I am a) in a terminal condition; b) permanently unconscious; or c) if I am minimally conscious but have irreversible brain damage and will never regain the ability to make decisions and express my wishes.

I direct that treatment be limited to measures to keep me comfortable and to relieve pain, including any pain that might occur by withholding or withdrawing treatment.

While I understand that I am not legally required to be specific about future treatments, if I am in the condition(s) described above I feel especially strongly about the following forms of treatment:

Cross out any statements that do not reflect your wishes

I do not want cardiac resuscitation (C.P.R.).
I do not want mechanical respiration.
I do not want tube feeding.
I do not want antibiotics.

However, I *do want* maximum pain relief, even if it may hasten my death.

Add personal instructions (if any)

These directions express my legal right to refuse treatment under federal and state law. I intend my instructions to be carried out, unless I have revoked them in a new writing or by clearly indicating that I have changed my mind.

Sign and date the document and print your address	Signed: _____ Date: _____ Address: _____
Witnessing procedure	I declare that the person who signed this document is personally known to me and appears to be of sound mind and acting of his or her own free will. He or she signed (or asked another to sign for him or her) this document in my presence.
Two witnesses must sign and print their addresses	Witness: _____ Address: _____
	Witness: _____ Address: _____

Counseling for School Children

Young people can be deeply affected by a serious illness in the family. School often becomes the focus of the children's stress. Many studies have shown that such children have difficulty concentrating on their lessons, with an accompanying decline in grade performance, and also have trouble relating to their peers. Others demand a great deal of attention from puzzled teachers who may never have been informed about the illness in the family.

Many communities offer counseling services for students from kindergarten through high school through the schools' guidance departments. You may wish to in-form the department about the illness in the family and the way in which your children relate to the situation. The counselor may be able to help identify emotional difficulties that adversely affect educational development and mental health. Through personal interviews, contact with teachers, and appropriate testing, the guidance department can assist children in coping with crisis, and refer the child to other professional agencies, support groups, or counselors if necessary.

Cystic Fibrosis

Cystic fibrosis is a disease that produces a thick mucus that clogs the lungs and digestive tract and literally starves and suffocates the body. An estimated ten million people are unknown carriers of the gene that causes the illness when it is expressed. There is no test to identify the gene; the only positive identification is when a child is born with it. There is no known cure. Children and young adults with cystic fibrosis undergo daily respirator therapy sessions to loosen the mucus clogging their lungs. For some, daily aerosol treatments are necessary to help their breathing.

The Cystic Fibrosis Foundation offers grants to biomedical research programs as well as support groups for patients and family and public education. In all these areas, the volunteer family member, relative, or friend—plays a vital role.

Contact:
Cystic Fibrosis Foundation
6931 Arlington Road
Bethesda, Maryland 20814
(800) 966-0444

Canadian Cystic Fibrosis Foundation
2221 Yonge Street
Suite 601
Toronto, Ontario M45 2B4

Financial Counseling

In the United States, for economic assistance and advice, look in your local telephone directory under "United States Government" for the appropriate federal agencies, such as:

—Office of Children (funds to help cover child care costs)
—Social Security Office
—Council on Aging or Elder Affairs Department

Emergency funds and facilities may also be available from your municipal or state department of social services. Consult your directory under "Social Services" and "Welfare Agencies."

Guidance and Family Associations

There is no greater stress for patient and family members than a serious illness. The lives of all concerned are changed profoundly. Guidance and family associations are there to help during these troubling times.

Family Service America, Inc. (FSA), founded in 1911, is an international nonprofit association dedicated to strengthening family life through services, education, and advocacy. FSA's almost 300 member agencies in the United States, Canada, and worldwide constitute the largest network of community-based counseling and support organizations for families. In North America alone, FAS serves more than 3.2 million families annually in over 1,000 communities.

Contact:

Family Service America, Inc.
11700 West Lake Park Drive
Milwaukee, Wisconsin 53224
(800) 221-2681

Recognizing the mental anguish that occurs during life-threatening illness, the Mental Health Association has brought together those who are ill and their families, community and professional groups, public officials, clergy, school, and employers. Over 350 mental health professionals identify unmet mental health needs, develop community resources and programs, and assist individuals in locating appropriate mental health services. There is a free information and referral line to help choose an appropriate counselor or therapist.

Contact:

Mental Health Association
7630 Little River Turnpike
Suite 206
Annandale, Virginia 22003

Professional social workers are trained to help families with life-challenging illnesses. Many work at guidance clinics and comprehensive health centers. Other therapists are in private practice.

Contact:

National Association of Social Workers
750 First Avenue, NE
Washington, D.C. 20002

The 1,200 chapters of the Information and Referral Service of the United Way of America aid those with terminal illness in finding appropriate support.

Contact:
United Way of America
701 North Fairfax Street
Alexandria, Virginia 22314

Heart Problems

The American Heart Association provides information about heart disease and specialized services for homemaking and home nursing, as well as facilities for heart patients.

Contact:
The American Heart Association
7272 Greenville Avenue
Dallas, Texas 75231
(800) 242-8721

Canadian Heart Associaton
1 Nichols Street
Suite 1200
Ottawa, Ontario K1N 7B7

Heart and Stroke Foundation of Canada
160 George Street
Suite 200
Ottawa, Ontario K1N 9M2

Home Care

Many seriously ill patients prefer to remain at home where warmth and familiarity replace the often cold impersonality of the hospital. Home health services provide skilled medical, nursing, and rehabilitation services. To ascertain the services available ask a hospital dismissal planner, hospital social worker, local or county health department, or family physician. Look in the Yellow Pages under "Nurses" or "Home Health Agencies." Medicare, Medicaid, private insurance, and other programs often pay for these services.

The American Health Care Association provides a state-by-state list of skilled nursing-home care and the specific services in each facility.

Contact:

American Health Care Association
1201 L Street, NW
Washington, D.C. 20005

Homemaking Service

Families need added support and care when a loved one is seriously ill. For food shopping, personal errands, light housekeeping, and assistance in hygienic duties, such as giving baths, changing dressings, and helping with prescribed exercises, consult your local telephone directory under "Homemaker" or "Home Service Aide," or contact your local social service department.

The National Homecaring Council is an organization that accredits homecare aides and grants national certification to homecare agencies.

Contact:

National Homecaring Council—
Foundation for Hospice and Homecare
513 C Street, NE
Washington, D.C. 20002

Hospice

"The purpose of hospice is to provide support and care for persons in the last phases of an incurable disease so that they can live as fully and comfortably as possible. Hospice affirms life and regards dying as a normal process. Hospice neither hastens nor postpones death. Hospice believes that through personalized services and a caring community, patients and families can attain the necessary preparation for a death that is satisfactory to them" (from NHO *Standards of a Hospice Program of Care*, November 1981).

Dame Cicely Saunders started the modern hospice movement in 1967, when she opened St. Christopher's Hospice in London. The first hospice in the United States was started in 1974 in New Haven, Connecticut. A comprehensive national survey by the National Hospice Organization recently identified more than 2,100 hospice programs in all fifty states and Puerto Rico.

Hospice refers to a coordinated interdisciplinary program of palliative and supportive services for terminally ill persons and their families. Programs vary in structure and state of development, ranging from interest groups to organizations that provide complete palliative and supportive services. Most programs provide home care and arrange for inpatient care when needed. Coverage of hospice costs is provided by Medicare and most Medicaid and private insurance programs.

Because a person is a composite of physical, psychological, social, and spiritual components, hospice care is often provided by a team in which these various disciplines are represented—most frequently, medicine, nursing, social work, and clergy. In addition, specially trained volunteers play an important role on the team. (See also Children's Hospice.)

Contact:

National Hospice Organization
1901 North Moore Street
Suite 901
Arlington, Virginia 22209

Canadian Palliative Care Association
5 Blackburn Avenue
Ottawa, Ontario A1N 8A2

Kidney Problems

The treatment of kidney patients is unique. Those with kidney failure must receive dialysis treatment or a kidney transplant in order to survive. Dialysis is generally required two to three times a week to cleanse toxic impurities from the blood. Transplant surgery and immuno-suppressant therapy necessitate constant follow-up care. Kidney patients are in continuous contact with their doctors and social workers.

Contact:

American Association of Kidney Patients
(800) 749-AAKP

The American Kidney Fund is a national, nonprofit, voluntary health organization providing direct financial aid to needy dialysis patients, transplant recipients, and donors to help cover treatment-related expenses. Grants are available to assist patients in affording medication, transportation, transient dialysis, special diets, etc. In addition, the Fund supports public and professional education, kidney donor development, and research. It publishes many brochures about kidney disease and its treatment, including selections in Spanish.

Contact:
American Kidney Fund
6110 Executive Boulevard
Suite 1010
Rockville, Maryland 20852
(800) 638-8299

The National Kidney Foundation is a voluntary health agency whose goal is to eradicate kidney disease and promote health services. Their projects include funding research, distributing educational materials, organizing seminars, sponsoring chapter newsletters, providing financial assistance on a limited basis, promoting professional education, and acting as a referral source.

Contact:
National Kidney Foundation
30 East 33d Street
New York, New York 10016
(800) 622-9010

Kidney Foundation of Canada
5160 Boulevard de Cary
Suite 780
Montreal, Quebec 83X 2S9

Lung Disease

The workings of the heart and lungs are interrelated. Blood travels through the lungs to be oxygenated each time it passes through the heart. If a clot forms in the blood vessel system and then travels through the bloodstream, it may eventually block an artery in the lungs, resulting in pulmonary embolism or death of tissue (infarction). Chronic lung disease can lead to heart failure.

Dedicated to the fight against lung disease, the American Lung Association (ALA) is the oldest nationwide, voluntary health organization. There are 115 state and local offices comprised of volunteers and staff that offer programs and educational services related to lung health. The associations also advocate for lung health and clean air, and support scientific research. The American Thoracic Society is the professional medical arm of the ALA, with state chapters throughout the country. They conduct workshops and training for lung disease sufferers on how to live with emphysema, chronic bronchitis, and asthma. Programs include Better Breathers clubs, advice on lifestyle changes, and training in special exercises.

Contact:

American Lung Association
1740 Broadway
New York, New York 10019
(800) LUNG-USA

Canadian Lung Association
1900 City Park Drive
Suite 508
Blair Business Park
Gloucester, Ontario K1J 1A3

Easter Seal Society
Suite 200
250 Ferrand Drive
Don Mills, Ontario M3C 3P2

Meals

There are various names for the service of meals to the homebound ill. Most common are Meals on Wheels and Mobile Meals; they may be found in the classified section of the telephone book. For further information,

Contact:
National Association of Meal Programs
101 North Alfred Street
Suite 202
Alexandria, Virginia 22314

Medical Second Opinions

As with all important issues in life, there may not always be agreement on medical procedures. One physician may recommend surgery; another may offer a totally different kind of treatment. What is essential to remember is that participation by the patient and family increases the chances of making the best medical decision. When a doctor suggests nonemergency surgery, consider obtaining another opinion. Getting another opinion is standard medical practice.

The United States Department of Health, Education, and Welfare recommends that if your physician suggests nonemergency surgery, you should ask him/her to give you the name of another doctor. If you would rather pursue the matter independently, you can contact your local medical society or medical schools for the names of the physicians who specialize in the particular field of illness.

If you are covered by Medicare you might call your local Social Security office or, if you are eligible for Medicaid, the local welfare office. For further information, call the U.S. government's toll-free number.

Contact:

Surgery
Department of Health, Education, and Welfare
(800) 638-6833

Multiple Sclerosis

Multiple sclerosis (MS) is a chronic disease of the central nervous system, which is typically diagnosed in people between the ages of twenty and forty—young people who are just starting their lives. About a third of a million Americans have MS. Women with the illness outnumber men two to one. All but a few people with MS can expect to live a normal life span, but many will do so with increasing levels of physical disability.

The National Multiple Sclerosis Society serves persons with MS, their families, health professionals, and the interested public. With more than 400,000 members, the Society provides funding for research, public and professional education, advocacy, and the design of rehabilitative and psychosocial programs. Direct services to individuals with MS are provided through more than 140 local chapters and branches. A Washington office is active in advocacy for federal legislation affecting people with MS, and in National Institutes of Health research funding. Chapters offer a variety of counseling and referral services; many offer group aquatics and other social/recreational support activities. Eighty-one clinical diagnostic and treatment centers are supported by chapters in twenty-five states.

Contact:

National Multiple Sclerosis Society
733 Third Avenue
New York, New York 10017
(800) 532-7667

Multiple Sclerosis Society of Canada
250 Bloor Street, East
Suite 1000
Toronto, Ontario M4W 3PG

Muscular Dystrophy

Muscular dystrophy is a progressive disease in which the muscle tissue decreases in size and grows weaker. In most cases the arms, legs, and spine become increasingly deformed. As of this edition, there is no cure. The best treatment regimen involves minimizing weakness through physical therapy.

Since its founding in 1950, the Muscular Dystrophy Association has provided comprehensive medical services to tens of thousands of people in hundreds of clinics across the nation. Its research program represents an effort to advance knowledge of this disease and to find cures and appropriate treatment. In addition, a professional educational program helps to increase knowledge and awareness of this neuromuscular problem among physicians, nurses, therapists, and the general public.

Contact:

Muscular Dystrophy Association
3300 East Sunrise Drive
Tucson, Arizona 85718

Muscular Dystrophy Association of Canada
150 Eglington Avenue, East
Suite 400
Toronto, Ontario M4P 1E8

Nurses

Nurses are often considered the real heroes in helping both patients and family. While both physicians and nurses provide health care, physicians may concentrate more on medical problems, while nurses focus on how the patient reacts to and deals with the problems, symptoms, and discomforts. To become a Registered Nurse (R.N.), one completes years of training in a university or hospital program and then passes a state licensing examination. Licensed Practical Nurses (L.P.N.'s) undergo a shorter and less academically oriented program than R.N.'s. Nurses' Aides are persons with less formal training who have learned their skills by working under the supervision of R.N.'s and L.P.N.'s. Patients with life-threatening illnesses and their families attest to the invaluable solicitude, care, and devotion by nurses of all kinds.

The more th .n 500 Visiting Nurses Associations in the United States provide a variety of home and hospital health care services in hospice and private duty. Check your telephone directory for your local health department, or

Contact:
Visiting Nurse Association of America
P.O. Box 100697
Denver, Colorado 80250
(800) 426-2547

•214

The National Resource Center of Kimberly Quality Care has more than 600 offices throughout the United States and Canada that provide information about home care, nursing services, and rehabilitation facilities.

Contact:
Kimberly Quality Care
90 Merrick Avenue
East Meadow, New York 11554
(800) 645-3633

Nutrition

Good nutrition is important for everyone. It is particularly crucial for those with life-threatening illness. Proper eating is vital to maintain stamina and mitigate the potential side effects of medications and therapies. Some diseases, such as diabetes, heart disease, hypertension, and various chronic gastrointestinal disorders, have a nutritional component. The dietitian trained in nutrition is the person to call for specialized regimens of food.

The American Dietetic Association is the largest group of nutrition professionals in the nation, and is open to those who meet its academic and experience requirements. Approximately 75 percent of its 64,000 members are registered dietitians (R.D.'s) who maintain the R.D. credential by meeting continuing education requirements. Additional members are educators, researchers, dietetic technicians, registered dietetic technicians (D.T.R.'s), and students. There are fifty state dietetic associations, plus those of the District of Columbia and Puerto Rico. Within these groups, there are approximately 220 district associations. A registered dietitian is a reliable, objective source of advice who can separate facts from fads, healthy meals from dangerous diets, and who knows how to translate the latest scientific findings about a serious illness into easy-to-understand nutritional information.

Contact:

American Dietetic Association
216 West Jackson Boulevard
Chicago, Illinois 60606
(800) 366-1655

Organ Donors and Tissue Transplantation

Organ transplants are medical miracles—truly gifts of life. As a result of technological advances, livers, hearts, kidneys, and a wide variety of other organs are now being transplanted. These operations are possible only when the needed organs are donated.

If you are willing to donate organs for use after your death, register as a designated organ donor. You might wish to discuss organ donation with your physician or local hospital administrator. Arrangements may be made either by executing a living will or, in some states, by having a notation added to your driver's license. In some cases, the pain of an impending death may be eased by arranging for an organ donation that saves the life of another person—or even, in some cases, the lives of several persons.

The Living Bank is the nation's largest multiple-organ donor registry and referral service. A nonprofit, nonmedical service organization, its goals are to find willing donors, coordinate the utilization of acceptable organs with medical facilities at the time of death, and explain organ donation. Its efforts are aimed at extending and enhancing lives; it is not a medical organization or storage facility. The Living Bank provides donor forms and cards which are legal documents in all fifty states under the Uniform Anatomical Gift Act. Donor forms are filed and information is kept on computer for reference at the time of death. The Living Bank has a twenty-four-hour referral service. Time is important in organ transplantation. The Living Bank should be called as soon as possible if death is imminent or has occurred. Quick notification of the Living Bank increases the chances of a successful transplant.

Contact:
The Living Bank
P.O. Box 6725
Houston, Texas 77265
(800) 528-2971

Multiple Organ and Retrieval Program of Canada
Toronto General Hospital
200 Elizabeth Street
Toronto, Ontario M56 2C4

Transplantation Services, the newest service of the Red Cross, collects, processes, and distributes tissue products. Tissues include cornea for sight, temporal bone for hearing, skin for burn patients, heart valves for heart defects, bone for orthopedic procedures, tendons and ligaments, and other tissues. These tissues help one-half million Americans each year to live more normal, productive lives.

In this new field of transplantation, the Red Cross is the nation's largest single organization committed to providing the safest and highest quality of tissue products. Transplantation Services objectives are:

—To distribute quality, lifesaving tissue products to those with disabling conditions.
—To educate the public and health professionals about the needs and benefits of transplantation.
—To train transplant technicians so that tissue is available for transplantation.

Contact:
The American Red Cross
17th and D Streets, NW
Washington, D.C. 20006

Canadian Red Cross Society
1800 Alta Vista Drive
Ottawa, Ontario K1G 4J5

Pain Control

The National Committee on the Treatment of Intractable Pain promotes education and research on more effective management and relief of unbearable pain.

Contact:
The National Committee on the
Treatment of Intractable Pain
c/o Mr. Wayne Coy, Jr.
1333 New Hampshire Avenue, NW
Washington, D.C. 20036

Physicians

A physician's knowledge of serious illness and appropriate treatment is invaluable. Earning the M.D. degree requires four years of medical school, and primary care physicians also train in their chosen specialty for three years. Further study is required for a subspecialty such as oncology or cardiology.

Family practice has been a specialty of its own with board certification since 1970. Family doctors are most familiar with the needs of the seriously ill patient and family. The American Academy of Family Physicians has more than 77,000 members in fifty states, Washington, D.C., Puerto Rico, the Virgin Islands, and Guam.

Contact:

American Academy of Family Physicians
8880 Ward Parkway
Kansas City, Missouri 64114

American Medical Association
515 North State Street
Chicago, Illinois 60610

Canadian Medical Society
1867 Alta Vista Drive
P.O. Box 8650
Ottawa, Ontario K1G 0G8

Psychological and Psychiatric Services

A psychologist is a person trained to deal with emotional issues such as the impact of illness on the patient and family. Most psychologists have an advanced degree (Ph.D.) and additional clinical internship training. Psychologists do not prescribe medications or perform physical examinations.

Contact:

American Psychological Association
750 First Avenue, NE
Washington, D.C. 20002

Canadian Psychological Association
730 Yonge Street
Toronto, Ontario M4Y 2BZ

A psychiatrist is a medical doctor (M.D.) who has completed a four-year course of study in a recognized medical school and four years of postgraduate training (residency) in the specialty of psychiatry. Because psychiatrists are physicians and trained in the use of drugs, they may prescribe medications for the seriously ill patient and, when necessary, for members of the family.

Contact:

American Psychiatric Association
1400 K Street, NW
Washington, D.C. 20005

Canadian Psychiatric Association
155–116 West Broadway
Vancouver, British Columbia V6J 5A4

A psychoanalyst is a psychiatrist who has highly specialized training in the field of psychoanalysis. Analysis is an intimate partnership in the course of which the patient becomes aware of the underlying sources of his or her difficulties, not simply intellectually, but emotionally, by reexperiencing them with the analyst.

Contact:

The American Psychoanalytic Association
309 East 49th Street
New York, New York 10017

The Canadian Psychoanalytic Association
7000 Cote des Merges
Montreal, Quebec H35 2C1

Rehabilitation

The goal of rehabilitation is to restore the patient to as normal a lifestyle as possible. It might entail retraining with an exercise program directed by a physical therapist, or help in learning how to use an artificial limb. The initial stage of rehabilitation may be started in the hospital, an outpatient center, or in the home. For physical therapy and rehabilitation, consult your telephone directory under "Rehabilitation Services," or

Contact:

American Physical Therapy Association
1111 North Fairfax Street
Alexandria, Virginia 33214

Canadian Rehabilitation Council
45 Sheppard Avenue
E Suite 801
Toronto, Ontario M2N 5W9

Religious Resources

The concerned religious community offers a society bound together by ties of sympathy, love, and mutual concern. Churches, synagogues, and other religious organizations can provide networks of meaningful relationships that can mean the difference between coping with or collapsing under the pressure of serious illness. Call your clergyperson, your church, synagogue, mosque, or temple, or

Contact:

American Association of Pastoral Counselors
3 West 29th Street
New York, New York 10001

Transportation

For assistance to patients who need to visit physicians or clinics when transportation is unavailable or inaccessible, contact your local social service department.

Women's Health Issues

For too long, women's health issues have been neglected by professional and legislative bodies. The National Women's Health Network is a public interest organization that provides current information on a variety of women's health matters.

Contact:
National Women's Health Network
514 10th Street, NW
Suite 400
Washington, D.C. 20004